Memento
A Coastal Recipe Treasure

By Maryanna Gabriel
Illustrations by Bly Kaye

Magic Cottage Creations & Trafford Publishing

Order this book online at www.trafford.com
or email orders@trafford.com

Most Trafford titles are also available at major online book retailers.

© Copyright 2009 Maryanna Gabriel.
All rights reserved. No part of this publication may be reproduced, stored in a retrieval system, or transmitted, in any form or by any means, electronic, mechanical, photocopying, recording, or otherwise, without the written prior permission of the author.

Note for Librarians: A cataloguing record for this book is available from Library and Archives Canada at www.collectionscanada.ca/amicus/index-e.html

Printed in Victoria, BC, Canada.

ISBN: 978-1-4251-86975

Our mission is to efficiently provide the world's finest, most comprehensive book publishing service, enabling every author to experience success. To find out how to publish your book, your way, and have it available worldwide, visit us online at www.trafford.com

Trafford rev. 8/5/2009

Design and layout by Maryanna Gabriel

Co-published by
Maryanna Gabriel
Magic Cottage Creations
www.MagicCottageCreations.com
& Trafford Publishing

 www.trafford.com

North America & international
toll-free: 1 888 232 4444 (USA & Canada)
phone: 250 383 6864 • fax: 812 355 4082

Table Of Contents

Beginnings......7

Lighter Fare..15

Entrées...........25

Loose Ends......41

Body & Soul....51

Acknowledgements

Special thanks to an editorial team extraordinaire whose input and suggestions have been invaluable: Naomi Rittberg, Brady Killough, Elodie Stauffer, Brian and Kathy Case, Lesley Delevett, Helen Rittberg, Yvonne MacKenzie, Genevieve Stonebridge, Leslie Gillett and very especially Susan Lagacé. Thank you to Jennie Rittberg, Maureen Milburne, and David and Nancy Wood for their support. You are all book angels. Lastly I wish to thank my cousin Bly Kaye for her lovely art and gentle encouragement for without her this book would never have happened.

Introduction

※

Here where I live waves lap the shore. Seaweed curls amid barnacles and driftwood while oysters cling to rocky beaches, the catch of the day awaiting in the ocean beyond. A thoughtful amble along country roads to the raucous sound of crows and gulls reveals red skinned tree limbs where Arbutus bark curls away like luscious chocolate. Inspiration from sea, land, and sky fuels a hunger deeper than the body as the soul savours quiet respite. Fulfilled, I turn homewards to a garden where plants find safe harbour behind fences from deer that love to nibble. By the wood fire a nurturing meal is enjoyed with loved ones and all is well.

This little book celebrates the beauty of where I live whilst cooking up a really good life. It is with this spirit that this collection of vegetarian and seafood recipes are offered. May it inspire you to do the same.

To You Whom I Love

Beginnings

Butternut Squash Dip

This absolutely delicious squash dip has a wonderfully unique and sweet flavour. To prepare, roast squash at 350° for approximately an hour depending on the size or until it is soft.

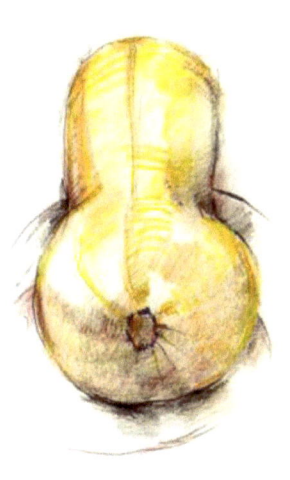

2 c. cooked Hubbard squash
3 cloves garlic
2 tbsp. cream cheese
3 tbsp. mayonnaise
1/4 finely diced Spanish onion
1/4 c. coriander
1/4 c. parsley
5 shakes of Tabasco
freshly ground pepper
2 tsp. chili powder
1 tsp. chipotle sauce
juice of one third of a lemon
1 1/2 tsp. teriyaki sauce

Mix the ingredients in a food processor and serve with your favourite crackers.

White Bean Dip

Mix the ingredients in a food processor until smooth. Adjust the seasoning to taste and serve with your favourite crackers.

1 c. white beans
1/4 c. fresh basil
4 tbsp. mayonnaise
2 tbsp. cream cheese
juice of half of a lemon
1/2 c. parsley
4 cloves garlic
2 tbsp. yogurt
6 drops Tabasco
salt, pepper

Mediterranean Antipasto

1 red pepper
1 green pepper
1 head of garlic
1 c. white beans
1/4 c. chopped artichoke hearts in oil
2 tbsp. chopped sun-dried tomato in oil
3 tbsp. chopped parsley, garlic chives
1 tbsp. chopped fresh oregano
1 green onion, minced
juice of a quarter of lemon
salt, pepper

Place garlic brushed with olive oil with the peppers and roast under a broiler. Turn the peppers until they have blackened, about 8 minutes each side, then lift the skin from the peppers. Slice the peppers very thinly lengthwise and place in a bowl. When the garlic is soft, squeeze from the skin. Add the remaining ingredients. There should be enough oil from the artichoke and sun-dried tomato for a dressing. Add lemon and season. Allow to marinate approximately 30 minutes. Serve with crackers.

Yam Zuni Rolls
With Raspberry Chipotle Sauce

This is an incredible combination of flavours that is exquisitely delicious.

Sauce

1 c. raspberries
1/4 c. port
1 tbsp. chipotles in adobo sauce
1 tbsp. sugar
1 tbsp. cornstarch

Combine raspberries, sugar, chipotles and port in a small sauce pan. Add starch to the sauce before warming, then slowly allow the sauce to thicken on a low heat.

Yam Zuni Rolls

One large baked yam
flour tortillas
Havarti Cheese
1 tbsp. butter
2 tbsp. cream cheese
1 tbsp. chopped parsley
2 tbsp. finely chopped scallion
salt, pepper

Scoop the yam out of the skin and place in a bowl. Add cream cheese, salt, pepper, chopped scallion and parsley. Combine ingredients with a fork. Grate Havarti onto a flour tortilla. Place yam mixture, log style, in the middle of the tortilla. Drizzle 1/4 tsp. of the sauce onto the mixture and roll the tortilla up. Warm butter in a frying pan and gently cook the tortilla seam side down until golden. This will seal it. Gently turn and cook until slightly golden on all sides. Remove and allow to cool somewhat and slice diagonally. Top each diagonal with sauce and dollop individually with sour cream.

Goat Cheese Walnut Dip
With Tortilla Strips

Goat Cheese Walnut Dip

package (5 oz.) goat cheese
2 tbsp. butter
½ cup walnuts
3-4 dashes Worcestershire
3-4 shakes Tabasco
½ tsp. curry powder
1 tbsp. plain yogurt
1 tsp. sour cream
cooking oil

Tortilla Strips

tortillas,
butter
parmesan

Gently toast the walnuts in a frying pan in butter for about 5 minutes. Add Worcestershire, Tabasco and curry powder. When the flavours are intermingled remove and allow to drain on a paper towel. Set pan aside leaving the traces of butter for later.

Soften the cheese with a fork together with the sour cream and yogurt until it is a smooth consistency. Mix in the toasted walnuts, setting a few aside for garnish. Remove the dip to an attractive bowl and surround with the toasted walnuts. Garnish with a sprig of parsley.

Cut tortillas into strips. In the frying pan heat butter and cooking oil on a medium heat and cook the strips a few at a time, turning as they brown. Sprinkle parmesan on them, it will melt into the tortillas. Remove to a basket and add freshly ground pepper. Serve with the dip.

Beet Latkes
(Serves 4)

I once assisted in the kitchen of a kibbutz and learned how to make these latkes which were eaten for both breakfast and dinner.

2 beets
1/2 minced onion
2 c. chopped spinach
2 tsp. baking powder
4 eggs
1 c. flour
cooking oil
salt
pepper

Wash the beets, cut off ends and then grate. There should be roughly 4 cups of loosely packed, grated raw beet. Place in a bowl with the onion and spinach. Beat the eggs and add the flour, baking powder and seasoning. Mix.

Form into thin patties and sauté, 2-5 minutes or until cooked through, depending on the size of the pattie, being careful to cook thoroughly.

Serve with the Wasabi Dip.

Wasabi Dip

This sauce may be used for whatever your imagination desires and is delicious with the latkes.

1/3 c. mayonnaise
1/4 c. plain yoghurt
2 tsp. wasabi
salt
pepper

Lighter Fare

Fried Clams
(Serves 2)

Steam one pound of clams and remove from their shells.

1 egg
1/2 c. milk
salt, pepper
1/4 c. bread or cracker crumbs
2 tbsp. flour
1 tbsp. cornmeal
3 tbsp. parmesan
1 tbsp. chopped parsley
chopped green onion
butter
cooking oil

In a bowl, mix egg, milk, salt and pepper. Mix in a blender or food processor: crumbs, flour, cornmeal, salt, pepper, parmesan and chopped parsley. Dip one clam at a time into milk and egg mixture and then into crumb mixture. In a frying pan place 6 tbsp. of cooking oil and 4 tbsp. of butter on medium heat. Cook until about 2-3 minutes or until golden and serve immediately topped with finely chopped green onion.

Steamed Mussels
(Serves 2)

1 pound mussels
1 c. water
1/2 c. dry white wine
1 tbsp. butter
garlic clove, sliced
half a dried chili pepper
1 bay leaf
10 pepper corns
1 tbsp. minced onion
1/4 tsp. chopped thyme
2 tbsp. chopped parsley
1 lemon

Simmer the ingredients, except the mussels, for 10 minutes. Add thoroughly scrubbed mussels. Cook covered for about 5 minutes until they have opened, discarding the mussels that have not opened. Divide between two bowls. Garnish with lemon wedges and chopped parsley. Delicious mopped up with fresh French bread.

Broccoli Cheese Soup
(Serves 8)

*C*hop vegetables and combine the ingredients and simmer until tender. Purée the soup.

1 pound of broccoli
(2 bunches)
6 c. water
3 vegetable cubes
2 cloves garlic
1 medium potato
1 carrot
1 small onion
1 tbsp. each of parsley, oregano, and garlic chives

Cheese Sauce

4 tbsp. butter
3 tbsp. flour
2 c. cream
3 c. grated orange cheddar
salt, pepper
1/2 tsp. dried mustard
1/2 tsp. Worcestershire Sauce
Tabasco to taste
1/2 c. dry white wine

*T*o prepare the cheese sauce melt the butter in a saucepan on a low heat. Add flour and stir until blended. Using a whisk stir in cream and remaining ingredients. Add the cheese sauce to the soup. Adjust seasoning. Garnish with saffron, croutons, chopped parsley, paprika, or with whatever

Crackers
(Makes 2 Dozen)

Well worth the effort, these crackers are perfect for most appetizers. To begin, place ingredients in a mixing bowl.

1 c. whole wheat flour
4 tbsp. sesame seeds
4 tbsp. grated parmesan
3 tbsp. shortening
1 tbsp. rosemary
1 1/2 tsp. salt
2- 3 tbsp. water

Cut in shortening until texture is mealy. Add water. Use corn meal and flour to prevent sticking and roll out until 1/8 of an inch thick. Cut with a diamond shaped cookie cutter and then cut each shape in half. Cook on an ungreased cookie sheet at 350° for 8-10 minutes. Cool on racks.

Naomi's Goat Cheese Bruschetta

Make crostini by brushing thin slices of a baguette with olive oil and then broiling until golden. Sauté onion in butter. When soft add Dijon and sugar until caramelized. Spread each crostini slice with goat cheese. In a mixing bowl toss together the caramelized onion, tomatoes and basil and place on the crostini. Finish with a thin slice of parmesan and fresh ground pepper. Broil until the parmesan melts, about 2-3 minutes, and serve hot.

1 loaf of your favourite baguette
1 package (5 oz.) goat cheese
1 Spanish onion thinly sliced
1 tbsp. sugar
1 tbsp. Dijon mustard
2 diced tomatoes
1 handful coarsely chopped basil
wedge of parmesan
pepper

Roasted Vegetable Salad
(Serves 2)

*G*arden vegetables are roasted with rosemary and parmesan and served on a bed of greens. This is a meal in itself.

On a baking sheet place sliced garlic, onion, and vegetables and coat the works with olive oil. Sprinkle with rosemary, coarse salt and pepper, and grated parmesan. Lightly drizzle with the balsamic vinegar reduction. Broil until slightly golden for approximately 6-10 minutes, then turn. Add more of the grated parmesan and broil for about 5-7 more minutes or until golden.

small slivered onion
sliced garlic
seasonal vegetables (about 1 cup per person)
salad greens
balsamic reduction (available at most grocery stores)
olive oil
rosemary
coarse salt
pepper
parmesan
goat cheese

Dress salad greens with your dressing of choice. Arrange the roasted vegetables on the top and garnish with goat cheese.

Zucchini Panini

Panini is Italian for "little breads". It may be served hot, cold, open-faced, closed, stuffed, topped, fried or grilled. This recipe is great picnic fare. Any bread may be used but thinly sliced focaccia or ciabatta (Italian breads) make wonderful panini.

focaccia or ciabatta
zucchini
portabello mushroom
eggplant
red pepper
onion
garlic butter
tapenaude
Fontina or Swiss cheese
mayonnaise
Dijon mustard
olive oil

Thinly slice, brush with olive oil, and grill or roast the vegetables using your judgement as to quantities, depending on how many panini you are making. Spread the bread slices with garlic butter, tapenaude, Dijon, mayonnaise, slices of cheese and then the vegetables. Grill the panini until toasted and serve with pickle and julienned carrots.

Oeufs D'Amour
(Serves 2)

4 eggs
2 tbsp. butter
2 tbsp. olive oil
4 tbsp. tomato sauce
1 chopped garlic clove
8 sliced mushrooms
2 tbsp. slivered onion
4 drops Tabasco
2 tsp. Worcestershire
1/4 c. grated cheddar
2 tbsp. parmesan
parsley
chives
salt, pepper

Butter two individual, small casserole dishes. Spread the bottom of each casserole with your favourite tomato sauce. Preheat oven to 350°. Melt butter in a frying pan and sauté garlic, mushrooms and onion. Add Tabasco, Worcestershire, salt, pepper and olive oil. Cook until browned. Place the mushroom mixture into the individual casserole dishes and break 2 eggs into each.

Top with cheddar, parsley, chives, parmesan, salt and pepper. Bake at 350° for approximately 12 minutes or until cooked through. Serve with toast.

Entrées

Halibut Tapenade For Two

Fresh halibut marinated in lime juice is smothered in a tapenade of black olives, capers and garlic and then broiled.

Finely chop or mix in a food processor:

12 black pitted olives
1 garlic clove
1 tbsp. capers
1 tbsp. white wine
15 peppers corns
(ground in a mortar to
a rough consistency)
1 tbsp. olive oil

Wash 2 halibut steaks and heavily juice with lime on both sides. Spread the steaks with the tapenade. Broil at 350° for 8-10 minutes or until white through. Serve with lime and chopped coriander.

Sole Fillets Wrapped In Basil
(Serves 2)

*S*ole is rolled with your choice of shrimp, crab or ground salmon. This impressive meal is easy to prepare.

6 sole fillets
1 c. shrimp, crab or ground salmon
3 tbsp. cream cheese
2 tbsp. mayonnaise
1/4 c. basil
parmesan
sour cream
salt, pepper, cayenne

Wash sole and douse with lemon juice. As if buttering bread, lightly spread each fillet with soft cream cheese and then mayonnaise. Top with freshly ground pepper. Place basil leaves on each fillet.

Place your choice of filling on one third of fillet and roll up. With the back of a spoon, lightly top with sour cream, parmesan, black pepper and cayenne. Bake at 350° until golden and white through, 10 - 15 minutes. Garnish with fresh basil.

Coquilles Des Isles
(Serves 2)

*C*oquilles is French for "shells". Scallops and mushrooms are brewed in a white wine sauce, then nestled into a bed of potato, and broiled "au gratin". To begin, boil and mash a potato, reserving the liquid and add the rest of the mashed potato ingredients as listed below and blend together.

Mashed Potato
1 potato
2 c. water
salt, pepper
paprika
1 tbsp. butter
1 tsp. grated parmesan
1 tbsp. Gruyère
1 tsp. capers
1 tbsp. cream cheese
1 tsp. chopped parsley
1 tsp. chopped green onion

Scallops and Mushrooms
Scallops for two (1- 1 1/2 c.)
1 tbsp. white wine
4 halved mushrooms
grated pepper
Tobasco
1 tbsp. chopped green onion
1 tbsp. chopped parsley
dash of fresh sage

Cream Sauce
1 tbsp. flour
1 tbsp. butter
scallop liquid
1/4 c. grated Gruyère
salt
pepper

Place 1 1/2 c. reserved liquid from the potato back into a skillet and simmer with the scallop and mushroom ingredients for 5 minutes or until tender. Strain and use the liquid for the cream sauce.

To make the cream sauce, melt the butter in a pot, add flour and blend. Add the liquid from the scallops and whisk until thickened then add the gruyere and seasoning. Combine with the scallop mixture. Place in shell shaped dishes. Surround the perimeter of the shell with the mashed potato. Sprinkle the top with bread crumbs, butter, Gruyère, paprika and a little green onion. Broil for 2-4 minutes or until golden.

Oysters Up A Rain Barrel
(Serves 2)

Oysters are stuffed into cannelloni shells and baked in a white sauce.

White Sauce

4 tbsp. butter
1 clove garlic
1/2 c. flour
1 1/2 c. milk
1/4 c. white wine
1 tsp. fresh thyme
salt, pepper
cayenne
1 tbsp. parmesan

Cannelloni

8 oz. oysters
cannelloni shells
(oven ready)
3 tbsp. butter
1 garlic clove
3 mushrooms
1 tbsp. red pepper
1 tbsp. onion
Tabasco
Worcestershire
1 tbsp. sage
1 tbsp. chives
1/2 c. cilantro
1/2 c. cottage cheese
1 c. bread crumbs
1 beaten egg
salt
pepper

Melt butter and cook with the minced garlic for a couple of minutes. Whisk in wine. Add milk, seasoning and blend.

Sauté the oysters in butter and garlic, cutting the oysters into small pieces in the pan. Finely chop mushrooms, onion, red pepper, and cilantro and add to the oysters together with the seasoning. Cook until the juices evaporate. Place in a bowl with bread crumbs, cottage cheese and the beaten egg. Stuff the cannelloni shells (around 10) with the mixture and position in a long, narrow, buttered casserole. Pour the sauce over the cannelloni. Top with cayenne, cilantro and parmesan. Bake covered at 350° for 45 minutes. Garnish.

Almond Salmon Torte
(Serves 2 - 3)

Crust
2/3 c. almonds
1/4 c. white flour
1/4 c. whole wheat flour
1/4 c. melted butter
1/4 tsp. salt
ground pepper
1/4 tsp. paprika
1/2 tsp. of curry powder

Filling
1 c. cooked salmon
3/4 c. bread crumbs
2/3 c. chopped vegetables
(mixture of carrot, green pepper, onion, celery)
2/3 c. grated cheddar
2 eggs
1/2 c. half and half cream
3/4 tsp. salt, ground pepper
parmesan
2 tbsp. mayonnaise
1/4 tsp. each of sage and dill

Mix the above ingredients in a food processor until fine. Cut in butter. Shape into a pie plate, patting the almond mixture with your hands and reserve a tablespoon of the crust mixture.

Mix salmon in a food processor. Set aside in a bowl. Add bread crumbs, chopped vegetables, sage and cheese. Next add eggs, cream, salt, pepper and mix in. Place the filling into the prepared almond pie shell. Top with dill, the reserved crumble and parmesan. Bake at 350° for approximately 25 minutes. Garnish.

Salmon Elodie Likes
(Serves 2)

Salmon is marinated with teriyaki and broiled.

2 salmon steaks or fillets
4 tbsp. teriyaki sauce
Dijon mustard
1 tbsp. brown sugar
1/2 tsp. dill
2 tbsp. onion
1 tbsp. sorrel (optional)
ground pepper

Place salmon in a foil lined baking pan and douse with teriyaki. Smother with a layer of mustard. Coat with a thin layer of brown sugar. Sprinkle with dill. Top with finely slivered onion, minced sorrel and freshly ground pepper. Allow to marinate for at least 15 minutes. Broil for approximately 10 minutes depending on the thickness of the salmon or until cooked through. If you serve the salmon with rice, polenta, couscous, or potatoes it is delicious served "au jus".

Yam Empañadas Stuffed With Shrimp
(Serves 4)

Savoury pastry with a yam and shrimp filling is rolled into small half-moon shapes, baked and served with a curry dip.

Dough
1 1/2 c. flour
3 tbsp. butter
1 tbsp. cream cheese
1 tsp. curry powder
ground pepper
1/4 tsp. paprika
2 tbsp. parmesan
1/4 c. cold water

Curry Dip
Add to 1 c. yoghurt: salt, pepper, curry powder and paprika to taste.

Cut butter and cream cheese into the flour and add the remaining dough ingredients and mix. Roll out and cut into circular shapes 2-4 inches in diameter.

Filling
1 c. baked yam
1/2 c. finely cubed mozzarella
1/2 - 2/3 c. of shrimp
2 tbsp. cream cheese
1/4 c. chopped parsley, celery leaf, chives
4 tbsp. chopped onion
1 tsp. basil
1/2 tsp. fennel
4 drops Tabasco
salt, pepper

Mash the yam and mix with the filling ingredients. Place a tablespoon onto one half of each circle and fold over so that it is a half moon shape. Pinch edges tightly. Bake at 350° for approximately 8 minutes or until golden. Serve with the curry dip.

Prawn Chilaquilies
(Serves 2)

This traditional Mexican dish is simple to prepare. Corn tortillas are sautéed then layered with potato, prawns, a zesty tomato sauce and cheese.

*8 corn tortillas
1 large potato
6-8 oz. prawns
1 1/2 c. tomato sauce
1 1/2 c. grated Monterey Jack
green onion
sour cream*

Thinly slice potato and parboil. Make tomato sauce. Cut tortillas into wide strips and brown in oil. Remove and drain on paper towels. In a lightly oiled casserole layer half the tortillas, potato, tomato sauce, cheese, chopped green onion and prawns. Top with tortillas, tomato sauce, green onion and cheese. Bake at 350° for no more than 15 minutes. Serve with sour cream.

Tomato Sauce

Purée in a blender:

*16 oz. plum tomatoes
1 small onion, chopped
1 garlic clove
1/2 c. parsley or coriander
Chipotle chilies to taste
for a wonderful, rich,
smoky flavour (accept no substitute).
salt
pepper*

Calamari
(Serves 2-4)

Calamari are no mystery to prepare and are delicious served with a Greek or Caesar Salad.

Tzatziki Sauce
(Serves 2-4)

1/4 c. to 1/2 c. yogurt
one minced garlic clove
1-2 tbsp. grated cucumber
salt, pepper, lemon, parsley
Mix and garnish with paprika.

Rinse and cut a pound of squid into rings. Pound to tenderize. Soak in lemon juice. Pat dry. Dredge in flour, salt, lemon pepper and oregano. Cook on a high heat in oil for 3-4 minutes or until golden then drain. Serve with the Tzatziki Sauce, wedges of lemon and minced parsley garnish.

Crab Cakes With Zucchini Salsa de Cielo
(Serves 2)

*H*eavenly is what cielo means and that is how these crab cakes taste.

Simmer the salsa, covered, for 30 minutes. In the interim prepare the crab cakes.

Crab Cakes

1/2 - 3/4 c. crab
2 tbsp. mayonnaise
1 beaten egg
2 tbsp. chopped red pepper
2 tbsp. chopped celery
2 tbsp. Spanish onion
1 minced jalapeño
1/2 - 3/4 c. flour
1 tsp. baking powder
salt, pepper

Zucchini Salsa de Cielo

1/2 c. finely diced zucchini
2 tbsp. chopped onion
1/4 c. finely diced red pepper
2 tbsp. raisins
1 jalapeño finely chopped
1 tsp. salt
6 tbsp. vinegar
4 tbsp. sugar
1 tbsp. coriander seeds
10 pepper corns

Combine the ingredients and form into patties. Sauté in vegetable oil for 4-6 minutes or until golden. Serve with the salsa.

Oyster Mushroom Couscous
(Serves 2)

Oysters are cooked with mushrooms and onions, into a rich gravy and served on a bed of couscous.

Oyster Mushroom Sauce

3 tbsp. butter
3 chopped garlic cloves
1/2 a small onion cut into wedges
10 halved mushrooms
3 tbsp. Worcestershire
1/2 pint of oysters (5-6)
1 dried crumbled chili pepper
2 tbsp. cream
1/4 c. mayonnaise
parsley, green onion

Couscous

1 1/2 cups of water
1 cup of couscous
salt and pepper

Melt butter in a frying pan. Add garlic, cloves, onions and mushrooms. Season. Allow to brown. Add Worcestershire and oysters cut into quarters. Cook on a medium heat for approximately 5 minutes. Crumble in dried chili peppers. Reduce heat. Add mayonnaise and cream. Allow to cook a few minutes more and serve on top of the couscous.

Place couscous and water in a saucepan. Bring to a gentle simmer and allow to cook for 4 minutes then turn heat off. Season. Place the oyster mushroom sauce on top and sprinkle with finely chopped parsley and green onion.

Ginger Grilled Halibut
(Serves 4)

Ginger subtly compliments this delicately flavoured white fish. This can be served with newly dug baby potatoes and a fresh green salad with chopped mint.

4 halibut steaks
1/2 c. orange juice
2 1/2 tsp. corn starch
1/4 c. teriyaki sauce
1 tbsp. maple syrup
2 tbsp. fresh ginger
1 green onion
ground pepper
cilantro
lime

Douse halibut with orange juice mixed with corn starch. Add the teriyaki sauce. Apply maple syrup to the top of the fish. Add slivers of ginger, diagonally slivered green onion, and some ground pepper. Grill or broil uncovered, spooning juice over the fish midway through cooking (approximately 8-10 minutes) and cook until the fish just turns white to the center. Garnish with chopped cilantro and lime.

Spinach Feta Pizza
(Serves 2-3)

Baby spinach, mushrooms, feta and garlic are served on a uniquely flavoured parmesan crust then topped with capers, cheeses and baked to perfection.

Crust

Mix in a bowl:

1 tbsp. fast rising yeast
3/4 c. warm water
1 tbsp. sugar
2 c. flour
1 tsp. salt
1/4 cup grated parmesan
3 tbsp. butter or shortening

Topping

cream cheese
mayonnaise
capers
pepper
oregano to taste
dried chili peppers
6 cloves garlic
Spanish onion
1-2 cups baby spinach

Adjust flour and knead together until elastic. Lightly oil the pizza pan and spread dough to the edges. Spread crust with softened cream cheese. Lightly top with a thin layer of mayonnaise. Sprinkle with thinly sliced garlic cloves, chopped oregano, chili peppers and freshly ground black pepper. Top with baby spinach leaves, capers, slivered onion. Crumble feta on top and finish with a generous sprinkling of Swiss cheese. Bake at 350° for about 10-15 minutes or until golden.

Tortilla Pie
(Serves 4)

Tortillas are layered with beans, corn, olives, onion, cheese, tomato and jalapeños. This is simple and easy to prepare.

4 tortillas
1/4 c. mixture of chopped onion and green pepper
1 chopped jalapeño
1 can of refried beans
1 small can of corn niblets
1 c. of grated cheddar
1/2 c. of tomato sauce

Butter a circular glass pie plate. Place a tortilla on the plate and spread it with tomato sauce, a layer of corn, chopped onion, green pepper and then cheese. Place another tortilla on top and spread with refried beans, chopped jalapeño and cheese. Layer with another tortilla and repeat the ingredients from the first layer. Place a fourth tortilla and top with tomato sauce and cheese.

Bake for 15 minutes in a 350° oven.

Nettle Crêpes
(Serves 4)

Nettles are loaded with essential minerals and are a tender delicacy, best gathered wearing rubber gloves in the early spring. This delicate dish is subtle in flavour and the nettles are delicious.

Crêpes

2 c. flour
4 eggs
4 1/2 c. milk
4 tbsp. oil
1/2 tsp. salt

Mix or blend ingredients. Carefully season the pan so crêpes remove easily. The art of making crêpes requires persistence and patience. This batter is for a very thin crêpe that does not need to be turned and makes approximately 12 crepes.

Filling

1 clove garlic
1 tsp. olive oil
2 tbsp. butter
1/4 c. chopped onion
1/4 c. chopped mushrooms
salt, pepper
1 c. steamed nettles
1 c. cottage cheese
2 tbsp. parmesan
sour cream
paprika
chopped chives

Wearing rubber gloves carefully gather nettles in a colander. Remove tough stems, chop and steam . Have no fear, there is no sting when the nettles are cooked. In a skillet mix olive oil, butter, garlic, mushrooms and onion and cook together until tender. Add salt, pepper and then nettles. Mix. Place the filling in a bowl and add cottage cheese and grated parmesan. Place approximately 2 tbsp. of filling on each crêpe and roll up. Put into a buttered casserole. Lightly spread sour cream over the crêpes with the back of a spoon. Sprinkle with parmesan, chives and paprika. Bake at 350º for 10 - 15 minutes or until hot.

Loose Ends

Jennie's Apple Pie

The cheddar topping is a delicious variation of an old classic.

Filling

5 apples peeled and chopped
2 tbsp. corn starch
1/2 c. brown sugar
a handful of raisins
cinnamon

Combine prepared apples and raisins; coat with corn starch and brown sugar. Sprinkle with cinnamon.

Topping

1/2 c. flour
1/2 c. white sugar
2 tbsp. butter
1 c. grated cheddar
dash cinnamon

Mix together flour and sugar. Cut in butter. Add cheese. Crumble the topping onto the pie. Add a dash of cinnamon. Bake at 350° until golden, about 45 minutes.

Crust

3/4 c. flour
1/4 c. oatmeal
1/4 c. shortening
1/8 c. cold water

To make the crust, mix the flour and oatmeal. Using a pastry blender cut in the shortening. Add water and form dough. Roll out the crust, place in the pie dish and add the apple filling.

English Muffins
(Makes 1 dozen)

3/4 c. warm water
2 tbsp. sugar
3 tsp. fast-rising yeast
2 tbsp. shortening
1 tsp. salt
2 c. flour
1/4 c. cornmeal

Place the warm water in a bowl and add sugar, yeast and stir. Add shortening and salt then stir again allowing the shortening to melt. Add flour and knead. Roll dough onto a floured board and cut into rounds. Allow to rise in a warm place until doubled (30-60 minutes). Brush each round lightly with water and roll in the cornmeal. Cook on a slow griddle in butter and cover with a lid for about 5 minutes or until golden and turn, adding more butter if needed, and cook for a minute or two more. These are delicious served buttery and hot with jelly or jam.

Lavender Biscotti
(Makes 2 Dozen)

3 c. flour
2/3 c. white sugar
3 tsp. baking powder
1/2 tsp. salt
1/2 c. pistachios
1/4 c. cut almonds
1 tsp. lavender flowers
zest of lemon
4 oz. chopped white chocolate
1/4 c. butter
3 eggs
1 tsp. almond flavouring

Add the wet ingredients to the dry ingredients. Oil hands to prevent dough from sticking and on an oiled cookie sheet form three logs. Decorate the top with a bit of brown sugar, grated lemon zest and some of the cut almonds. Bake at 325° for 25 minutes or until golden. Cool slightly. Slice the logs a half inch thick, on the diagonal. Place on the baking sheet; do not crowd. Return to a cooler oven of 225° and bake for another 20 minutes until crunchy. Store in an airtight container.

Tisane

1 sprig lemon balm
1 sprig sage
honey

This is a French word meaning a herbal or floral infusion of tea. Lemon balm, it is written, has calming properties. Sage is reputedly good for soothing the soul and is said to relieve "night sweats". Tie together and steep.

Mountain Cookies
(Makes 18 Cookies)

*T*oast the almonds in the oven at 300° for approximately 8-10 minutes and then blend the butter and the sugars.

Add to the butter and sugar misture:
1 egg
1 tsp. vanilla
1 c. flour
1 tsp. baking powder
1 1/2 c. rolled oats
1 c. almonds
4 squares (16 oz.) of chopped chocolate
1/2 c. dried cranberries

In a large bowl blend:

1/2 c. butter
1/2 c. brown sugar
1/2 c. white sugar

Roll into 1 1/2 inch balls and flatten with a fork. Bake at 350° for 12 minutes or until golden on the bottom.

Chai
(Serves 2)

*I*t is easy to make this deep, creamy, rich tasting tea of spices and milk which may be taken hot or cold. Chai is reputed to have been made over 5,000 years ago.

2 c. water
1 c. milk
2 teabags or 2 tbsp. dark tea leaves
1 cinnamon stick
4 whole cardamom pods
6 cloves
6 peppercorns
4 tsp. sugar or to taste
1 tsp. sliced fresh ginger

Add water to a small sauce pan. Gently grind spices in a mortar and pestle and then add to the water along with the sugar. Allow to boil uncovered for 5 minutes. Reduce to a simmer and add tea then milk and heat. When steeped, strain into a pot or cups and serve.

Wild Rose Jelly

Gather wild rose flowers when they bloom in late spring.

4 c. wild roses (loosely packed
6 c. rose water
2 tbsp. fresh lemon juice
1 box pectin crystals
8 c. sugar

Simmer the blossoms in water for 10 minutes and strain. In a large saucepan bring the liquid, and pectin to a boil. Add sugar and lemon juice. Return to a hard boil for one minute (when the liquid runs off a spoon in a "sheet" it is jelly).

This fey ambrosia is magical because the dark juice the flowers yield turns pink with the addition of lemon.

Pour into sterilized jars and seal.

Plum Chutney

Combine sugar and vinegar. Add remaining ingredients. Mix well and bring to a boil. Reduce heat and cook stirring constantly for approximately 12-15 minutes or until thickened. Pour into hot sterilized jars and seal.

3 c. chopped plums
1 c. chopped pears
2 1/2 c. white sugar
1 c. vinegar
1/4 c. chopped onion
4 minced scallions
2 chili peppers
1 c. raisins
1 tbsp. salt
12 cloves
1 tbsp. cardamom
1 tbsp. mustard seeds
1 tbsp. whole coriander
2 tbsp. freshly grated ginger
4 cloves minced garlic

Blackberry Vinegar

This vinegar may be mixed with olive oil into a vinaigrette and served on a bed of greens. It may also be used as a marinade for fish or fowl.

1 c. balsamic vinegar
1 c. blackberry juice
1 sliced garlic clove
sliced fresh ginger
10 peppercorns

Combine the ingredients and place in an attractive bottle.

Body and Soul

Face Mask

This is guaranteed to nourish the skin.

In a blender mix:

an egg white, a handful of raw oatmeal with any one of the following:

a huge strawberry,
half of an avocado,
a chunk of cucumber.

Add any combination of these herbs:

mint
(skin pick-me-up)
lemon balm
(smoothes wrinkled skin)
comfrey
(promotes healthy skin)
yarrow
(inhibits spider veins).

When puréed, spread the tonic over the face and leave for 10 or 15 minutes. The skin will experience a pleasant tingling sensation. Wash off, pat dry and soothe skin with your favourite moisturizer.

Hair Rinse

Combine any mixture of sage, nettles, rosemary (for sheen), chamomile and yarrow (to lighten) in water and simmer lightly for 10 minutes. Strain. Combine five parts of the infusion to one part apple vinegar. This will make your hair feel silky and very soft.

Massage Oil

Peanut oil is reputed to be a preventative measure against arthritis. The therapeutic benefits of massage of others or self are numerous. Ylang-ylang is an essential oil from flowers in tropical Asia and is used in aromatherapy to create languid calm.

6 drops of ylang-ylang
1 c. peanut oil

Milk and Honey Bubble Bath

*I*t is written that Cleopatra bathed in milk and honey. This bath is silky and smooth for skin. To prepare, warm the ingredients and blend. Pouring into the running water increases the foam. Sink into the bath and feel like royalty.

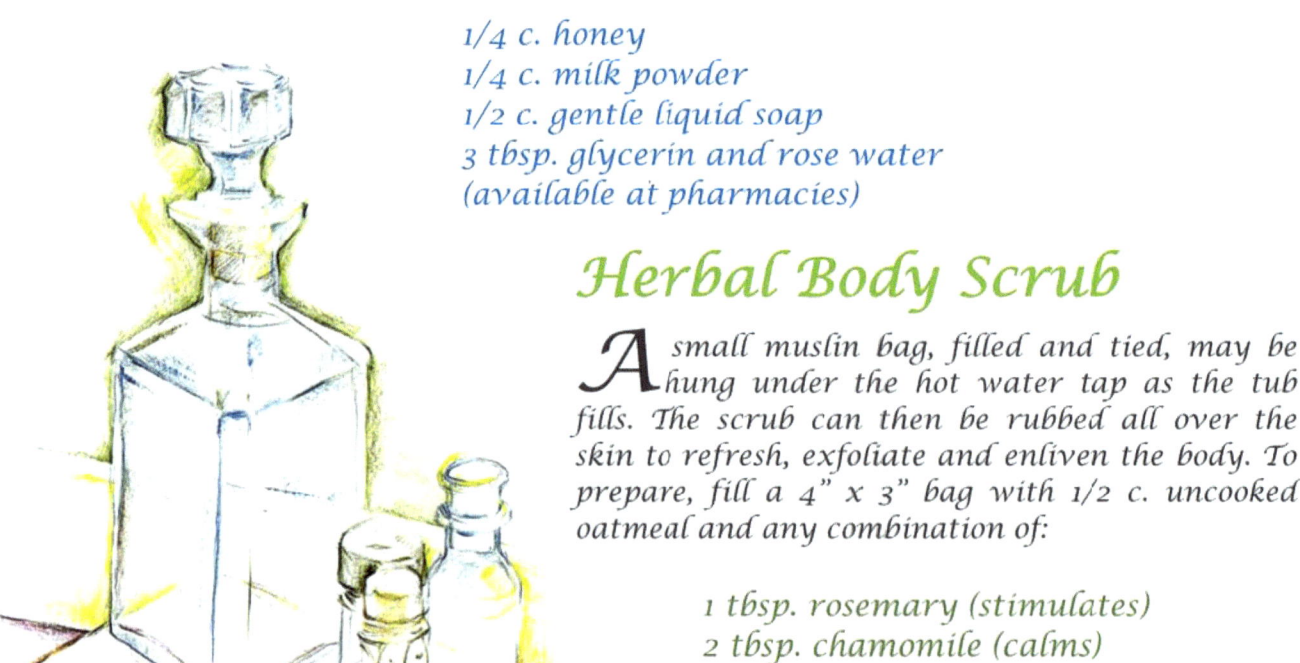

1/4 c. honey
1/4 c. milk powder
1/2 c. gentle liquid soap
3 tbsp. glycerin and rose water
(available at pharmacies)

Herbal Body Scrub

A small muslin bag, filled and tied, may be hung under the hot water tap as the tub fills. The scrub can then be rubbed all over the skin to refresh, exfoliate and enliven the body. To prepare, fill a 4" x 3" bag with 1/2 c. uncooked oatmeal and any combination of:

1 tbsp. rosemary (stimulates)
2 tbsp. chamomile (calms)
1 tbsp. peppermint (refreshes)
1 tbsp. daisy (promotes cheer)
2 tbsp. lovage (deodorizes)

Coastal Tonic

In a mixer combine:

An ocean breeze
A chorus of frogs
The cry of the eagle
Light sparkles
from ocean waves
The curve
of the cormorant
The scent of fir
A pinch of salt
A hint of spring

Blend. Drink in deeply.

Breathe.

Spiritual Invigorator

*P*atiently prepare:
 1 c. gratitude
 1/2 c. generosity
 2 c. forgiveness
 1 c. humour

Playfully roll with the punches and mix thoroughly. While minding your own business spice with each of a:

 pinch of honesty (maybe 2 pinches)
 sprinkle of peace
 and a dollop of joy to taste.

Mix considerately with hope and a murmur of prayer. Buttering up the pan with acceptance prevents sticking. Bake with attitude in a temperate oven and when it springs back, wisely let it rest. In the interim, a sugar topping greatly enhances the flavour. Serve with love in your own way and in your own time.

Index

Almond Salmon Torte	30	Face Mask	52
Beet Latkes	14	Fried Clams	16
Blackberry Vinegar	50	Ginger Grilled Halibut	37
Broccoli Cheese Soup	18	Goat Cheese Walnut Dip	13
Butternut Squash Dip	9	Hair Rinse	53
Calamari	34	Halibut Tapenade For Two	26
Chai	47	Herbal Body Scrub	9
Coastal Tonic	55	Jennie's Apple Pie	43
Coquilles Des Isles	28	Lavender Biscotti	45
Crab Cakes	35	Massage Oil	53
Crackers	19	Mediterranean Antipasto	11
English Muffins	44	Milk and Honey Bubble Bath	54

Index

Mountain Cookies	46	Spinach Feta Pizza	38
Naomi's Goat Cheese Bruschetta	20	Spiritual Invigorator	56
Nettle Crepes	40	Steamed Mussels	17
Oeufs D'Amour	24	Tisane	45
Oyster Mushroom Couscous	36	Tortilla Pie	39
Oysters Up A Rain Barrel	29	Tortilla Strips	17
Plum Chutney	49	Yam Empanadas	32
Prawn Chilaquilies	33	Yam Zuni Rolls	12
Raspberry Chipotle Sauce	16	White Bean Dip	10
Roasted Vegetable Salad	21	Wild Rose Jelly	48
Salmon Elodie Likes	31	Zucchini Panini	23
Sole Fillets Wrapped In Basil	27	Zucchini Salsa De Cielo	35

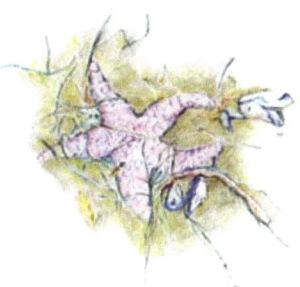

About The Author

Maryanna Gabriel's passion for food is attributed to her parents and family where good cooking is considered a religious experience. She is often asked, "Did you really make these recipes up?" The answer is yes with the caveat that some are inspired by friends and travels. A graduate from Simon Fraser University with a Bachelor Of Interdisciplinary Studies (Archaeology Minor), Maryanna also holds a Library Technician Diploma, a Legal Secretary Diploma and a Certificate In Fine Arts from Emily Carr University. She is the business owner of *Magic Cottage Creations* where she works in graphic art, advertising, writing, photography, and marketing. Born in Montreal, Maryanna has lived across Canada but primarily on Canada's west coast. She is an avid cook, adventurer, traveller, kayaker, gardener, artist, and mother of two amazing daughters.

Photograph by Genevieve Stonebridge.

About The Artist

Helen Bly Kaye was born in Montreal, Quebec, into a family with extensive artistic roots and in her early teens moved to the Okanagan in British Columbia. After a year at Neuchatel Junior College in Switzerland she graduated from the Vancouver School of Art (now Emily Carr University) and studied education at the University of British Columbia. Bly frequently teaches and her art is in galleries and private collections in British Columbia and across Canada. She lives with her husband, Garry, on Salt Spring Island where both work as full time artists and where she is continuously inspired by the world around her.

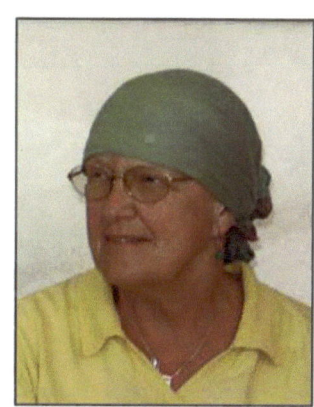

Photograph by Garry Kaye.

www.ingramcontent.com/pod-product-compliance
Lightning Source LLC
Chambersburg PA
CBHW042017080426
42735CB00002B/88